The Great Small Business Plateau^{SM}

Patrick Lee

TABLE OF CONTENTS

Forward

I hate business consultants. What do they know? Have they ever actually run a business? Do they have a clue what I am dealing with?

Many small business owners like me have little time for business consultants because – frankly - business theory is easy, getting it done is what is hard. So very hard. Against this all too familiar backdrop I stumbled across Patrick Lee, introduced to me as, yes you guessed it, a business consultant. Like many small business owners I am not an easy prospect. Quick to judge, slow to listen. Yet years later I am still relying on Patrick to help grow my business and can pinpoint how he moved me from one path to a much more fun and exciting path that I, my wife and kids, and my bank manager are all enjoying more than ever before. Life is great and I would not have gotten here without Patrick's guidance. That simple.

I was asked "What makes Patrick different?". Unlike other business consultants, he doesn't come with cheesy anagrams of the five steps to success. He doesn't have a complicated process to keep him gainfully employed at your expense. He doesn't try and impress you with his resume or achievements. He simply offers you access to one of the most energetic, insightful, creative brains I have come across in over 25 years of business. He understands people as much as he understands business.

Patrick is really not a business consultant. He is considered the horse whisperer for us stubborn, smart, experienced and tired small business owners. He listens. Prods. Soothes. Listens. Prods. Listens. Then he helps you see a much more colorful, holistic, exciting picture of your own life, your own business, your motivations and your opportunities. It's like somebody opening the blinds in a dark room. His brilliance lights up your mind so that you can decide what you want to do. Then he keeps going and helps you map out the way to get there.

As business owners we like making money. Patrick helped me to see in what ways I was helping drive profits, but also in what ways I was slowing down profit growth. He also helped me verbalize which aspects of the business I enjoyed and which ones I didn't like (and wasn't particularly good at). Connecting all these dots into a concrete business plan requires a powerful business brain. That is what he offers.

This book is long overdue. I wish I had read this 10 years ago. This book will not only show you how you can grow your business, but also how to do so in alignment with your personal values, motivations, and goals. Patrick's insights will help move you from feeling tired, stressed, and worrying about growth to having a peace and excitement about each day of your life. The path he offers will help your business blossom without the stress and without feeling tired.

I hate business consultants. Patrick "the business owner whisperer" is an exception worth your time.

Leo Brenninkmeyer, client: 2013 – today.
Founder, Compass Languages

Dedication

To My Parents
Karren and Patrick
Without your guidance, I would not have the thirst for knowledge nor the zeal for entrepreneurship

In memory of Alan Bechtold
1953-2015
Rest In Peace

Acknowledgements

First and foremost, I need to thank Sandy Wilmore and Anne Hartig for their help in editing this manuscript. Without their assistance all would have been lost.

I need to thank Bob Regnerus for coordinating everything related to the publishing of this book and for his inexhaustible patience.

I would be remiss if I didn't express my gratitude to those individuals who have allowed their stories to be told in these pages.

I am also indebted to my Spark compatriots, Kathryn Collings Laing, Suzette Langley, Dave Cyphers, Stephen Etzine, John Leitch and Theresa Connelly.

Last, and definitely not least, I need to thank my family for their exuberance about this project and their continually pushing me to get this book finished.

The cover photo was taken by Michelle Wilson.

eBook & print design by John Daily, Elysian Press.

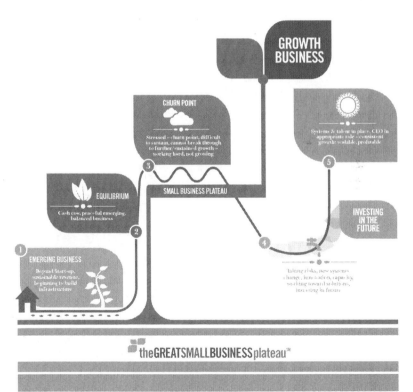

GROWTH BUSINESS

CHURN POINT
Stressed – churn point, difficult to sustain, cannot break through to further/sustained growth – working hard, not growing

Systems & talent in place, CEO in appropriate role – consistent growth: scalable, profitable

EQUILIBRIUM
Cash cow, peaceful emerging, balanced business

SMALL BUSINESS PLATEAU

INVESTING IN THE FUTURE

EMERGING BUSINESS
Beyond Start-up, sustainable revenue, beginning to build infrastructure

Taking risks, new systems change, innovation, rapidly, working toward solutions, investing in future

theGREATSMALLBUSINESSplateau™

© 2015 The Spark Business Institute

9

INTRODUCTION

Most entrepreneurs will tell you, in those moments of extreme introspection, that if not for the allure of significant rewards, no one would ever bother to launch or run a business. There are too many seemingly endless 24/7 weeks involved in the start-up phase, followed by ever more work to be done to build and grow the business. No one in his or her right mind would ever take on such a challenge without the potential of significant rewards and a desire to create. The size of those rewards – even after going through all the work and sweat to collect them – largely depends on certain decisions that happen along the way. The hard work at startup alone is not enough.

One of the most difficult decisions you must begin with is figuring out the kind of business you want to build. Everyone knows the type (think industry) of business they want to start. What is frequently overlooked is what kind of business they are going to build. Is the business going to constantly grow and reinvent itself so it is always expanding? Or is the business going to grow to a predetermined size and then maintain itself at that level?

You might think you can simply start a business and see where it takes you. In fact, most business owners do exactly this, but making a conscious decision between two basic kinds of businesses, high growth or lifestyle, is vitally important. Do you want to build a solid, stable lifestyle company that will keep you comfortable for the rest of your life? The lifestyle approach to business is one where you build by design or inherent limitations, to a predetermined revenue and infrastructure size. When you are satisfied with where you are, and the rewards are adequate, you simply maintain that level. Content with the amount of money the business is generating and not interested in additional risk, the goal is to achieve only the minimal growth necessary to maintain stability at this desired level.

Do you dream of building and taking your small company to large-company revenues? If you approach business with a high growth mentality, prepare yourself to continually strive to build upon current revenues by 15, 25, and even 100 percent over a set period of time. Deciding between the two, lifestyle vs. high growth, is important, because after the startup phase, when the business gets rolling and is profitable, almost every business reaches a plateau – a point where the business could grow to the next level and revenues could skyrocket, but not without significant changes. These changes require risk and are therefore often anxiety inducing challenges. If the need for change is not addressed, businesses at this phase typically struggle and eventually stall. It's at this point where you will see the value of having already made the decision about the kind of business you're building, or you will find yourself needing to make this determination while under extreme duress.

Understanding the kind of business you're running, or which kind of business you are best suited to run, is essential to meeting your ultimate goals and will be invaluable in addressing the inevitable plateau successfully – to move your business through its next development phase. Even if your goal is to maintain a lifestyle business, you will need to make subtle changes to keep up with personal, economic, and market factors necessary to sustaining your company. The ideal scenario requires a business owner who carefully plans for these factors and periodically analyzes the health of all aspects of the business, including its revenue goals, financial situation, product/service viability, infrastructure, and short and long term marketing plans. The vantage point of an outside advisor is often necessary to help walk through this complex process and make choices best suited to the business' specific situation to avoid getting caught on the plateau or, if you are already there, negotiate past it to build a successful venture.

Most business advisors recognize that there are revenue levels upon which developing businesses will frequently pause, before continuing to grow. If this pause becomes protracted, despite the best efforts of the businesses' leaders, the business has reached The Great Small Business Plateau^{SM}. It becomes clear that something different is needed to move the business forward, but it is rarely clear to the management team exactly what. Companies beyond 10-15 million in annual revenue have a vast array of specialized consultants and advisors at hand to serve them and help them work through their troublesome phases. Companies in the 1-10 million revenue arena, however, remain vastly underserved. Think back to when you were a startup. You probably had access to a lot of resources for the initial phase of your business, but finding experienced, qualified help navigating troublesome phases thereafter was likely difficult. This lack of readily available and qualified expertise is despite a clear need; in my experience, nine out of ten companies in this demographic will hit the plateau and will not get past it without some form of help.

I wrote this book to help business owners facing The Great Small Business Plateau^{SM} understand the symptoms and reasons for this condition and to begin an exploration of ways to prepare and get past the plateau with the best possible outcome. If you're building or running a lifestyle business, I offer ways to get your business to the point of ideal equilibrium – that place where the long-term revenue you need is firmly in place and reasonably secure and your profits are maximized, your efficiency laudable. If you are building or running a high growth company, I offer ways to identify where the plateau lies for you, and to apply the necessary strategies to move forward and grow your business into even more profitability than you originally imagined.

By following the principles outlined in this book, you'll have a much better chance of building the kind of business you're striving for, in almost any economic situation. I urge you to use this information as a guidepost, to help you recognize the decisions that you will need to make in order to achieve your stated goals.

The Lifestyle Vs. High Growth Choice

Regardless of your choice of kind of business, both lifestyle and high growth companies can experience The Great Small Business Plateau^SM. Lifestyle companies operate with the primary intention of a select few getting the most out of the company – often this is the owner and/or partners. Typically, the owner has a set of skills upon which the entire company is based. This owner, as only one person, has a limited productive capacity and knows he or she would have to do even more for the company to grow and flourish. Even with herculean effort, the company can only grow so far before being limited by the capacity of the owner. If the company were to add an additional specialist to the mix, capacity would increase, but there's still a cap on the potential growth rate because the entire vision of the company is limited by the owner's singular viewpoint.

Complicating the issue is that even successful lifestyle businesses don't operate in isolation of the economy and market. Economies and markets change and so must lifestyle companies, even if just to stay on pace with cost of living and market trends. As a result, owners, decision makers, and shareholders must plan ahead or stay abreast of these trending factors and their impact on the viability of the business. Neglecting to consider these factors can result in slow deterioration of the lifestyle model through diminishing profits and/or declining revenue.

In contrast, high growth companies are continually looking to increase their capacity. As they run out of excess capacity, they re-adjust, so that money coming into the business begins to fuel necessary capacity expansions and keeps the business moving forward. Imagine it like this: your company is currently worth 2 million and you want to be worth 20 million in three years and 100 million in five. In order to get there, you are going to have to fuel your high growth in ways you never before thought possible or even likely, constantly assessing and reassessing all aspects of your business. Failure to do so will not position your company to weather the natural dips and plateaus in revenue growth in the long run. To produce the true high growth we're talking about here, you have to think big and plan and plan and plan. It can feel a lot like the painful startup phase of the company, but if you are not constantly moving forward, you will plateau.

The Great Small Business Plateau^{SM}

Companies naturally mature as they progress. The initial startup phase is followed by a period of growth, where you may or may not realize the business' equilibrium point. The equilibrium point is where the business is at its most efficient for its current systems and capacity. It is during this period that the company becomes a true going concern. It is also somewhere during this phase that the plateau creeps up and surprises many businesses.

Most often, businesses that hit the plateau are already well-established, small or medium sized entities. So, what does a plateaued business look like day-to-day? It is often profitable; therefore the owners find themselves taking fewer risks and making minimal reinvestments as the focus shifts to keeping current revenues stable. As revenue growth begins to slow down, or even decline, owners allow their past business experience and gut instinct to fully determine their decisions and become complacent with their market standing. Sometimes, an owner will try multiple initiatives in order to grow past this plateau, all to no avail. The initiatives are frequently based on the owner's now outdated vision and lack of an accurate, current analysis. The expense of these initiatives frequently puts a strain on the company's ability to maintain its current levels. Reserves begin to decline. It takes more and more effort and resources just to stay at current levels. This is the churn point, marking a company's arrival at the plateau.

Businesses will experience plateaus for different internal and external reasons. If not diligently monitored, there are many inhibitors to a business' continued success and growth. These growth inhibitors include misalignment of an owner's motivations, goals and behaviors, limited personnel skill sets, outdated marketing plans, as well as inadequate or obsolete infrastructure, products, services, and technology.

It is easiest to identify where the growth is stalled in your specific business by obtaining and tracking data, then performing a detailed analysis of the numbers you're seeing. When you run the right numbers and know what to look for, you can spot these trends and know, with reasonable certainty, when you're about to face a plateau. These signs generally show themselves well ahead of the actual growth downturn and combine, over time, to create that plateau. Once you have identified a precipitating event(s), you can begin investigating ways to move the business forward. An outside expert can help you target which change will offer the best return on investment. This is critical because whether it's necessary or not, any change – such as changing your product or service, your infrastructure, how you interact with your customers, consolidating your customer base, increased competition, or changing industry – can chip away slowly at profitability and growth, if the change isn't managed correctly and with consistent objectives in mind. This is the risk that often keeps an owner from making any change or from making additional changes after an initial attempt fails.

Unfortunately, changing a business and creating entirely new systems and capacity isn't a direct lateral move (see the diagram of The Great Small Business Plateau[SM] on page 9). Instead, it normally forms a slingshot-like curve and involves a scary downtrend. You'll naturally have cash flow issues, stressors, personnel changes, and other challenges inherent in any attempt at radical change within a stable organization. In the move to grow, these challenges will exhibit themselves in almost every area of your business. Major change requires tenacity, diligence, and confidence.

It's here, on the downward curve, where trouble often lurks. The majority of business owners, remembering the monolithic effort required during their startup phase and being uncomfortable with risking the security of the status quo, are not prepared to handle the sensation of taking a step backwards. They're already fighting to stay at the plateau level, where they have grown accustomed to the size of their business and what this requires and provides. As the diagram illustrates, getting past the plateau usually results in a dip in profits and/or revenue and includes other business stressors. This is a curve that feels unnatural – dangerous, even. In truth, any downward motion that is part of the steps toward growing through the plateau can and should be determined and planned for ahead of time to ensure that these stressors are temporary. This is where extensive and knowledgeable coaching and mentoring is needed, but all too often such help is either unavailable or unwanted by the owner of the stressed small and midsize business. Faced with going it alone, most business owners choose to try to stay where they are – stuck, at best!

With the right support and systemic change, however, businesses can break through the slump and take off again, shooting back up and growing – this time with greater capacity and numbers than they had before. With the help of an advisor, owners can lay out the benchmarks and prepare stakeholders for navigating the inevitable change curve.

Transitioning off the plateau - by creating additional capacity, creating entirely new systems, and jumping back into growth - without proper guidance can be more stressful than any other phase of building a business. The truth is, moving beyond the plateau does involve some risks and it feels risky doing it. To be successful, you have to consider all the forces inhibiting growth.

On one hand, you may be able to rediscover your business' natural equilibrium point and adjust the business to create the efficiencies necessary to thrive there. This is where you acknowledge that you prefer a lifestyle business and make efforts to optimize your current systems and create the best outcomes for your current business model. You might, however, consider making drastic changes to move your business back into high growth, such as selling all or part of the company or merging with another successful company.

Sometimes this type of tactic, unnatural as it may feel, can enable you to expand the business, by adding services and product lines, introducing your products into new profitable markets, and making it possible for you to reach into new geographic regions. To most small business owners, a move such as an acquisition or sale might sound intimidating, but it could actually prove to be the best way to achieve continued growth for you and everyone involved in your business. In any case, failure to adequately prepare and act with intention can easily result in the business staying at a churn point until the bitter end.

You might think businesses, which are based on cutting-edge innovations, would be immune to this slow-down. They aren't. Even in the best of circumstances, internal factors such as personnel changes or incompatibility, infrastructure or business capacity limitations, as well as external factors such as changing market demographics, can bring about plateaus of their own. Macro-economic factors like recessions can and often do bring about plateaus in businesses. These inhibitors force owners out of their comfort zones to make changes in their operations in the hope of overcoming or riding out their stalled growth. Most often the plateau does not lead to this type of systemic change, although it should. Unlike the rapid downward force of a recession, the plateau is often a slow and insipid downward pressure.

It's important to remember, however, that implementing change, in and of itself, does not necessarily enable a business to make it through a plateau. You must make the right changes for your particular business to realize success.

The analysis of business metrics, market research, and goals and objectives, often proves key in determining what changes are required to achieve the desired business state. This data can even warn you of the plateau before it arrives. It can show you ways to take your company straight through the plateau and on to rapid, steady high growth.

The upcoming pages tell the stories of companies who evaluated their growth inhibiting factors. Most business plateau scenarios involve multiple inhibitors that require deep analysis beginning with the founders' vision. With strategic interventions, most were able to prepare or revise their business plans and move their companies forward.

CovingtonAlsina I: Identifying Growth Inhibitors

Ann Alsina started her wealth management firm, CovingtonAlsina, in July of 2012. Shortly after starting the company, she joined one of the private advisory boards of which I was the Chair. "I was in financial planning with a different firm before that," Ann says. "I owned my book of business, but I didn't own the firm or have any control." Ann told me she always appreciated my business knowledge and acumen, but she initially sought me out for help with accountability, clarifying of focus, and to get ongoing feedback.

Part of Ann's motivation for starting her own firm was her desire for control. There were several differences in values between her and the owners of the previous firm. She also wanted to build something she could eventually sell. "A main obstacle from the start was financial," Ann explains. "Another obstacle was administrative - getting the paperwork done and staying on top of everything. It was overwhelming. I had to let my assistant go shortly after we started because she required too much supervision to be a real help. When I was ready to hire a new assistant, there was a whole lot I hadn't yet considered."

CovingtonAlsina's business plateau was a compilation of several inhibiting factors, starting with Founder's Cap, an owner's limiting vision of undefined target markets and the tendency to create self-limiting approaches to business development. This was complicated by the Jack-of-all-Trades Mentality which interfered in Ann's ability to delegate tasks to competent staff members. In short, Ann was stuck in survival mode, instead of thriving in growth mode. The more you're caught in the little details, the less you can focus on realizing the vision. Ann says, "After I joined the private advisory board, we really started to work on my business, versus working in my business. Working in my business helps me pay my bills every month. Working on my business helps me grow my business and build it. They're very distinct."

In order to address Ann's business challenges and move her company through the plateau, I told her I thought there was another piece she and I needed to address, before we tackled the personnel issues that she attributed to causing her plateau: we needed to align her motivations with her behaviors. Why did she want to embark on a new path? What did she want to accomplish with this new endeavor? Even if she had the optimum employee situation, a business cannot flourish if the owner's goals and aspirations are not aligned with the business plan, market demand, and day-to-day operational needs. We met, and she started putting forth her goals, of how much she wanted to be worth, when she wanted to retire, and what doors she wanted to open. I realized it was probably going to be very difficult for Ann as a small financial planner to achieve her high growth goals– even in the best of circumstances. Business owners like Ann need to make sure that what they do aligns with what they say they want – and it works in both directions. In Ann's case, she was being ambitious in her thinking, but didn't have the structure to accomplish her objectives. In most cases, it's the other way around. A business owner might have the capacity to do more, but their motivations aren't really aligned with high growth. Their behaviors are often more about lifestyle needs than their business' growth needs.

I told Ann we needed to back up a bit and first align what she could accomplish with her operation, with what she said she wanted to accomplish. Ann said this was hard for her to answer. "Since I've always worked in financial industries, I tend to talk money. I want this many clients. I'm going to make this much revenue. I want to grow it to this size."

I pointed out to her, "You say those things, but what you really talk about is taking care of your clients and giving back to your community. Those are your values. It's a different mindset from your talk of money."

Ann's motivations and her desires truly were for a high growth business. She figured once she got her business going and profitable, she could explore her philanthropic vision, which included serving specific clients and other organizations in her community. Her success would naturally lead to her having greater impact on her philanthropic endeavors. The problem was when we looked at her operations, she was stuck in survival mode. Her chances of ever achieving those desires weren't really high. Ann is just one among a few hundred competitors offering similar services, just in her local area. There are severe limits on a business that has a saturated market like this. What she didn't have was a clear vision of what she could offer an already saturated financial planning market that would make her business stand above the rest.

The Founder's Cap

Aligning personal goals with a business vision is critical to keeping a company growing. Often business owners will find themselves with this Founder's Cap, one of the fundamental inhibitors to growth. Businesses experiencing the Founder's Cap, and there are many, fail to thrive to the level the owners envision. Although not always the case, a large majority of the people leading small businesses are the founders.

Businesses develop, because founders/owners have an idea that culminates in a company being formed. These individuals are successful enough to get their business past the startup phase and to turn an initial profit. Now their business is a going concern, they have employees, clients, revenue, and hence obligations. They've garnered a significant amount of attention for their business success. They're proud of what they've accomplished. Even though they work extremely hard in their business and not necessarily on the business, they're ultimately the smartest individual at the business. When you learn how the founder looks at the market and the business world, you'll quickly find that everything – including the business' ability to grow – is centered on the founder's understanding and expertise within their niche market, their ability to solve problems, and their ability to make sound decisions. These business owners are notorious at being micromanagers. You won't find a great number of people in their companies empowered to make decisions or do anything without first running it by the founder. Instead, they tend to employ people who are only empowered to gather important information and act on it when they're directly instructed to do so by the founder. Employees are not there to provide additional capacity in the form of expertise beyond the founder, but are there to support the founder.

As a business owner or founder, there's a point you'll inevitably reach when you realize that what got you to where you are isn't going to take you to the next level. If you want your business to keep growing, you will need to open yourself up to learning new skills, to trying new ideas, and to be continuously evolving.

Some founders are primarily driven by their egos. They thrive on the attention that comes with owning their own business. They get to make important financial decisions. People must speak to them to seriously discuss any aspect of the business venture. They are the engine that makes it all go. Being in the spotlight is just one of the perks of being a business owner – but it's an important one to this particular type of owner. Making all the important decisions is one of the main things you get to do as a owner, and many people truly love being in this kind of power position.

Realize, however, that this type of owner will often hesitate to shake things up and turn over the reins to anyone else in any capacity, seeing it as a threat to the ego boost they get by running the business themselves. Without a serious wake-up call, this type of founder will often wind up going down with the business (worst case scenario), or being constrained to very limited and very frustrating growth efforts (best case scenario).

The Founder's Motivations vs. The Organization's Vision

At one point in time, I was asked to serve on the board of a nonprofit which worked with special needs children and adults. The organization's vision offered a pristine picture of what the future could be for these individuals, but it wasn't attaining the reach and high growth needed to help as many people as it could. I was drawn to the cause because I have a child with special needs who was already utilizing the program. Thinking it would be a great opportunity to volunteer for a worthy cause, I accepted the position.

Once on the board, I was immediately struck by how different things were on the inside than what I had observed from the outside. The founder of the organization had stepped aside, leaving her spouse to run it. While there was tremendous potential for the organization to help a lot of people, that potential needed to be unleashed. I was put in charge of strategic planning. The founder claimed to want to take the organization to a new level in order to have a bigger impact on the community it served. It was just a matter of how to go about making that happen.

After a year of multiple attempts at strategic planning, it was revealed that underneath the founder's loftier stated vision, her actual goal was to build a new facility. While a new facility would have provided personal benefit to the founder, it would not have had notable impact on achieving the much loftier vision. Many volunteers and board members had invested a great deal of time and energy attempting to realize a vision they believed in, only to discover that the real purpose of the nonprofit was to support the founder's hobby. Consequently, the entire board resigned. While the founder eventually got her new facility, the organization never achieved its full potential in either size or scope.

CovingtonAlsina II: Differentiation

Recognizing Ann's motivation was a key factor that needed to be addressed at CovingtonAlsina. By asking Ann to reevaluate her business goals and her niche, I was hoping to help her identify and build a unique service in her market, something that differentiated Ann from all the other financial planners. Ann determined she indeed wanted to build a high growth business. Once the vision was set, we settled in to work on refining her service offering – how was CovingtonAlsina unique? I asked Ann, "What gap is there? You have to identify the gap in your industry and figure out how you can fill it?" This struck a chord and Ann knew immediately what I was talking about.

"In the financial planning industry," she said, "most everybody wants clients with 3 to 5 million in assets. Those are considered high-net-worth clients. Once you get clients with more than 10 million, it's ultra-high-net-worth. If you get to 20 million and above, those people generally aren't served by a traditional firm; they're served by what's called a multi-family office. It comes from the idea of a 'Family Office' – which is what the Rockefellers have – that manages all their trusts and personal wealth. Someone with 20 million dollars, however, still doesn't have enough money to warrant running an office on their own, so there are multi-family offices that deal with a handful of these very wealthy families, catering to their every whim and handling all their business needs."

Ann continued, "People with between 3 and 10 million net worth that's not liquid, however, are wealthier than 99% of all Americans – but they can't use it right now. At the same time, they're making good income. Still, most advisors don't want to deal with somebody with money they can't invest, because you don't earn any real money handling their accounts. That's a huge unfilled need. At that level of net worth, they have no time whatsoever; they're working 60-80 hours a week. It's an opportunity to serve them now and tell them, 'The ultra-wealthy have a multi-family office. Let's do that now – for you."

"To do this for them, we would have to be able to provide advice and investment information, coordinating everything for them like a multi-family office – now. Then, when they have those liquidity events later, there's a nice big payout, in terms of investable assets. With Patrick's help, we identified this gap in the marketplace. From that gap – I just had to go find those clients who fall into that niche."

Ann knew the gap was there, but never thought about it as a business opportunity. She reports it doesn't narrow her client base at all, because she can still service her current clients and decide when and if she will take on a client who doesn't meet her niche demographic. Ann and I did research, and just in her county alone, she couldn't begin to handle a significant percentage of people in the target demographic. What a great future growth opportunity for her company!

Jack-of-all-Trades Mentality

Another behavior that inhibits business productivity is called the Jack-of-all-Trades Mentality. Ann's initial comments to me about being overwhelmed with managing the organization and administrative pieces of the business led me to also suspect the Jack-of–all-Trades Mentality was holding her business hostage.

The Jack-of-all-Trades may be the owner or an employee. This person or persons are able to do a bit of everything in the company, but are not necessarily experts at any one task. Founders often haven't hired, nor are they actively seeking, to bring anyone into the business who is smarter than they are in any one area. They figure they can manage the various jobs themselves, or they've reached out and found key people for the company who are highly competent, but may not be especially gifted in specific areas. In the end, these people wind up serving as the founder's support staff – which means they support the founder's brilliance without necessarily enhancing or expanding it.

For example, let's say a founder decides the business needs someone who can handle recruiting new hires. A member of the founder's current support staff will almost always respond that they're the best choice to handle the human resource needs of the company. Since the founder is already paying this staff, the feeling is that the existing employee may as well be used to handle recruiting and hiring. Neither the owner, nor the staff, may have the necessary skills to do this job really, really well. Compromised recruiting and hiring leads to compromised employees.

In another example, let's say the business has a growing number of clients to serve and keep happy, and in order to continue to grow, the founder considers hiring someone to help with servicing these clients. The dilemma this founder faces is that he or she is personally familiar with their clients. He or she knows them well and works with them, knowing how to best service them. He or she already has a personal connection. Founders find it difficult to justify any additional expense. Why bring in someone new to the game when you can shuffle around existing employees already capable of handling it all for you? By using someone who is already familiar with the business and all that it has to offer to deal with clients, Jack-of-all-Trades reasoning says that you're using your resources to their fullest. There's no reason to spend money bringing in new staff members when you can use the assets you currently have, correct? Wrong! In this example, you and your staff have become competent at everything, but specialists in nothing.

Founders Cap and Jacks-of-all-Trades Mentality are just two of the inhibitors to business success. A third inhibitor is infrastructure inadequacies. Infrastructure includes all aspects of a business operation that go into creating and producing a product or service: personnel, space, equipment, and production/service technology. Additionally, there are administrative tasks for each of these areas. In general, tasks include all the requirements that go into every sale, including internal and external communications and the coordination of work. The office needs to be competently staffed and managed. Phone calls have to be made. Files have to be organized. E-mails need to be answered and paperwork has to be completed. The impact of inadequate personnel and technology systems are rarely taken into full account. There are always setbacks such as sick days, computer problems, or extreme weather conditions that cut capacity – even company politics can put a stick into the wheel. Usually, none of this is fully calculated into the efficiency of producing a profit.

The Personnel Inhibitor

This takes me back to the initial reason Ann came to me for help. Her Jack-of-all-Trades perspective was not going to allow her to meet the needs of her clients. She needed to re-evaluate who she had on staff to help her. She had an assistant, but like many business owners in her position she had an unwieldy amount of work dependent upon that assistant. This is a formula for burning out staff. To build for high growth, you have to find the right people as you start out, so you can expand their abilities and not end up with only generalist staff contributing only marginally. These key personnel decisions are where trouble begins for most founders and owners. It's one of the issues that is stopping your business from getting to where you want it to be. If you're going to get beyond the plateau and take things to the next level, you need to understand how your current key personnel and any new hires you bring on board are working for you. Identify what you're going to be able to accomplish with them, beyond what you can accomplish on your own. In short, what area of expertise does each staff member contribute.

The key here is not hiring reactively. Many times, someone will show up on your radar who is available, and seems far too good to be true. You might think they're more talented than anyone you've ever hired for the organization and here they are, available to work for your company! You start thinking you can pull a few strings, overlook some apparent weaknesses, make some concessions, and get them to work for your organization. You're in a hurry to get the right people in place anyway, so you skip doing the kind of due diligence needed for hires at this level.

You end up making the hire. You tell yourself you were lucky to get this person. In reality, you chose this person because you were in a hurry, they looked better than you expected to find, and they were immediately available. This isn't at all the best approach for the organization – especially when you take into account the plateau and the need to push past it – but it happens too often. There's an old adage that a business should determine the job description before hiring, not create a job description around a hire. This is almost always true.

Like all aspects of running a business, hiring should be strategic, because an employee's highest productivity, potential, and possibilities cap the organization's ability to grow. It caps it just as effectively as an owner's insistence on doing everything as a Jack-of-all-Trades. Hiring strictly for the purpose of supporting the founder will only support limited growth. A founder might be good at everything, but that doesn't mean there aren't any areas that could be made even better with the application of specialized knowledge and experience. It can and will make the difference between a business department that's performing extremely well or just adequately. Adequate performance, as we've already discussed, won't help blast you past a plateau and into high growth.

By strategically adding specialized personnel, you can leap past the plateau much more readily, reassured by the fact that your key personnel are even more capable, and smarter in their specialties, than you could ever be. The first couple of key personnel you hire for your business can, as we've seen, present you with a painful set of decisions. Many people feel they have to get it right quickly and if they don't, everything is doomed to fail. All this can indeed make those first few key hires a difficult jump for business owners and founders to undertake.

To get past this inhibitor, you need to recognize that not every hire is going to be perfect, but the individual you're considering just might have the expertise to expand your capacity in order to take your business to new levels – even though they aren't as versatile as the Jack-of-all-Trades.

You might have a company that has multiple positions where key personnel are needed – but you're not comfortable with the cost of bringing them in all at once. In this situation, you need to ask which areas will have the most impact for moving the business forward – which key position or two, properly filled with smart people who have specialized skills, will allow you to grow, and therefore be able to hire additional key personnel in the future.

CovingtonAlsina III: Hiring Key Personnel

Ann knew she at least needed an assistant to handle paperwork, so she started the process of advertising for a new employee. When the applications came in and she started interviewing, she liked one person, but she thought they might experience significant friction working together. I suggested we do some personality assessments. I already had Ann's assessment results on file. We had the top three candidates complete assessments, which gave Ann a great overview of their working styles and how they would work with her – critical information for hiring successfully. It turns out that the candidate she thought would drive her batty probably would have. The other two both would work well, in terms of personality.

The personality assessments we used, examined employer-employee relationships and how perceptions might contribute to compatibility – positively or negatively. They assessed how the candidates would perceive Ann's management style and ways in which she might perceive their behaviors – as well as better ways for everyone to work together and communicate. "That's been helpful in terms of the person I did hire," Ann says. "To be able to say, up front, 'this looks like it's going to be an issue, are you good with this approach?'"

It's not just hiring the right employee, it's also having in place a development plan for that person. It's knowing what they're going to need to learn and when. What other skills do you believe their position will require? Are you going to send them off to practice public speaking? Or, are you going to send them off to learn how to use Microsoft Excel? What are you going to do to ensure that they're on a constant growth path that parallels how their specific skill set will need to be expanded as the company grows? Also, can you assess when they are at full productive capacity? For example, you find you need IT expertise and none of your current personnel fit the bill. How will you determine if you can afford to hire an IT specialist or if you have to cut a position to hire this expertise? How do you assess when to train and when to hire?

You must be very deliberate about what you aim to achieve. Otherwise, you will just continue accumulating employees and building relationships with people you may like, but who are lacking specialized skill sets. Your loyalty to them also means that you may be unable to make a change, even when it is necessary. It is these employees who are limiting the business' growth potential by possessing adequate supporting skills, but very few, if any, specialized skills.

Ann realized this was the case with her assistant and she realized she needed expert help in a few other areas in order for her business to meet the needs of her new clients. She alone couldn't provide all of the expertise for a multi-family office that serves investment management, legal estate trusts, tax planning, asset protection and concierge services. She also couldn't afford to hire someone for each of these areas, so one of the things we looked at was building alliances with other professionals to provide these services on an as needed basis. Outsourcing is a perfectly valid way of bringing in expertise and expanding the business' capacity. But, if you want that expertise from people, who are really connected and contributing as part of your organization, and identify with the business' values, you're going to have to go beyond the standard quid pro quo, collaborative arrangement. These collaborators need to come in and be part of the planning process for each of the clients and they've got to be vested in the company brand, so much so, that they want their clients to be a part of it, too.

Ann now has one other advisor who works at CovingtonAlsina and she's a 1099. She owns her own book of clients, but by working with the firm, she uses the CovingtonAlsina company name, agrees to use its processes and investment options, and Ann gets a portion of all her new business. As opposed to hiring, Ann is able to set up strategic alliances to bring in additional skill sets on a collaborative basis.

In general, without mapping out human resource capacities, it's easy for business owners to become too optimistic, saying they are capable of handling 50 clients within a three-month time period when, in reality, they might not be able to handle anywhere near that number. Without considering this data, an owner can inflate the business' perceived capacity, but in reality, this overestimation of potential may end up costing the business due to poor customer service, unrealized opportunities, and finally, business lag.

Ann came up with very creative solutions to these challenges. She doesn't have to pay everyone out of pocket and the resulting collaboration is beneficial to everybody involved. Ann recognized that the potential of her business would be limited to the services she, herself, could provide, unless she was willing to hire and collaborate. "My time is still split," Ann reports. "Obviously, to keep the business going, I still have to meet with clients. Having a staff person who's qualified and is coming along quickly has freed me up from a lot of the admin tasks that I previously was responsible for and had to do. The time I'm spending in my business is more productive and profitable as a result."

In the end, Ann and I identified several barriers which contributed to the lull in CovingtonAlsina's business growth. Despite the initial complaint being personnel inadequacies, the actual inhibitors ended up including a misaligned founder's personal and business vision and growth goals, and a saturated product market, which impacted personnel needs and consumer demand. Presently, Ann is spending much more time laying out the planning and the groundwork for launching her newly focused firm to fill the market gaps we identified in order to grow to the level of her ambitions.

The Infrastructure Inhibitor

Identifying a business' inhibitors to growth is critical to moving beyond the plateau. As explained, inhibitors can be internal, external or some combination of both. CovingtonAlsina's business and many others are hampered by both, but sometimes a business' growth plateaus because its infrastructure isn't sufficient.

Take for instance the example of one veterinary blood bank. The practice moved into a 3,300 square-foot center with several other veterinary specialty practices. Each practice had its own office and the treatment area was shared. The practices flourished and soon outgrew the space. When the center's landlords were approached about the need for a larger space, they failed to see the need, arguing that no patients had ever been turned away for lack of space. They were completely unaware that there was in fact a strain on cage space, waiting lists for the surgical suites, and a shortage of staff to handle the number of patients. Staff had become adept at making do and being functional even if not optimal. High quality requires resources, in this case space and staffing, to deliver its promise.

When you look at it on the surface, it's understandable you might not realize the impact that limited space and infrastructure can have on your ability to grow. It can be vitally important that you expand at the right time, before you're out of capacity. If you wait, you risk hitting a wall and going into stop-gap mode, trying to keep the opportunity of expansion alive even after demand has already started declining.

Over the course of time, the landlords of the center, where the blood bank was located, became convinced that expansion was necessary. Another property was purchased and three-and-a-half-years after construction began, the practices moved into a new 10,500 square foot space with ample parking. Unfortunately, by the time they moved in, they'd already outgrown the new space and were entirely unaware that this would turn out to be the case.

There wasn't much thought put into the cap that had already existed on the previous 3,300 square-foot building. Because of the space limitations that existed, a veterinarian would examine a sick dog and consider hospitalizing it and running some diagnostic tests, but since space was so limited, the veterinarian would simply draw some blood, run some tests, and send the dog home. The landlords hadn't realized this was already going on well before the move and continued immediately after the move, despite the additional space. They had underestimated the reality of the size of the built up demand. In addition, they made the mistake of not recognizing that their caseload was continually growing - so they outgrew 3,300 and needed 10,500, but didn't take into account that patient growth was continuing to increase during the 3 year interval while they were building and would continue to increase - they were building to meet existing demand and not adequately planning for future demand.

Three years after moving into the new space, the success of the blood bank made it necessary for them to move into a separate facility. The space that had been allocated to them, in the 10,500 square foot building, was now far too small for them to operate efficiently and realize their full potential.

This is how it often goes with founders and their businesses. No one realizes the opportunity until after it happens. Small business owners wait for the increase in demand to happen before making major changes. They figure they'll take care of something when enough people come in and ask for it. The fact is that, as the movie Field of Dreams says: more often than not, if you build it, they will come. Don't wait for enough business to come to you before taking action to grow. The market demand is searching for a supply source. You want to be that source. By the time you accept that it's real and do the necessary steps to build appropriate capacity, the demand may have found another source. Opportunity doesn't wait around.

As a small business owner, this is one of the biggest calculated risks you'll need to take to blast past the plateau. As a startup, you took your concept out of the gate. You launched a business and, despite all the odds against it, created a sustainable company. Once you get to a perceived secure point in your venture, however, it becomes harder and harder to put that security at risk and go after high growth.

Trying to be both secure and adventurous is very difficult. They are natural enemies of each other. Mitigating risk is wise, but avoiding risk is limiting. By fully understanding the importance of opportunity building and the philosophy behind, "if we build it, they will come," you open up the possibilities of high growth.

Entering Into a New Market

Another infrastructure consideration is the expansion of your products' offerings. You can kick growth into high gear by finding an identifiable gap in a known industry's market. If you're the first one to start filling the gap, you can reap a majority of the rewards. But you absolutely must study the market you intend to enter, to make certain what you can offer will be a fit.

Richard owned a construction company and had invented a patented masonry product. He put it onto the market, and it was a hit – his "big thing" had happened. Richard's company was profitable and he was making great money – but then the pressure was on. The company had hit its plateau. It dominated the market it was designed to fill and there wasn't much room left for growth. Richard decided to invent another product, one that would solve a problem that no other product could. This is a valid path to expansion. If you can create something that fills a genuinely underserved or inadequately solved problem in the market, especially in market space that you understand, it could work well.

Richard came up with a new product. It was similar to the one he'd invented for use with masonry, but was directed towards a different type of construction. The whole time he was working diligently to create this new spin-off product, he was thinking there has to be a demand for his new creation. After all, the original product worked fine - people were buying it steadily. He figured his new product would be just as popular as the previous one, but for a different segment of the building market.

Richard's new product worked, so he patented it, started producing it, and then sat back and waited for the sales to pour in. They did not. The problem was, Richard failed to do the analysis and planning that should precede diving into the creation of any new product. No significant research was conducted on the market for the product he was planning to release. He figured the product would be sold in one specific sub-market that he was somewhat familiar with, and essentially designed it with that sub-market in mind.

The second problem that Richard unknowingly stumbled into was an overinvestment in the new unproven product. For his first product, he outsourced most of the production, keeping overhead and infrastructure costs to a minimum. He didn't own the production facilities for the product. Even though he distributed the item and held the patent, the item was being produced in some other company's factory. But for this new product, Richard decided he wanted to own the means of production, so he invested $150,000 in all the equipment to manufacture the item. He made additional investments to secure a location for the equipment and to hire the personnel to keep it running. Richard was so certain he had another hit in the making that he invested all this money and got everything ready to roll, then waited for the magic to happen.

This is when I came into the picture. The product was released and the marketing cranked up. It didn't do a thing. It fell completely flat. Initially, Richard thought it was a problem with the product's performance. Next he suspected a problem with the way the product was being marketed. The lack of sales didn't have anything to do with the product, the distributors, or the marketing push behind the product. It was actually a market problem. Richard wanted to market the product to the West Coast, but the industry had no use for the product there. No one was ever going to use it. They didn't even have a reason to think about buying the product, because it addressed an issue that they simply did not encounter.

The move proved to be a complete mistake on Richard's part because he failed to prove that there was a need for the product in his target market area. Still, it was a good product and it was patented, with an infrastructure investment to produce it. To recover the research and development costs, investment costs, and to successfully bring the product to market, I was handed the situation and asked to fix it.

I conducted the market analyses that should have been done initially, and found a market for the product. The size of this specific market was far smaller than what Richard had originally hoped for, so reverse engineering needs had to be considered: different profit structure, production changes, and everything else that goes into a complete infrastructure retooling. But it was still potentially profitable and provided him a chance to recoup his losses, but eventually added very little towards real sizable growth for the company. It did, however, take up a bunch of time, energy, and capital that could have been earmarked for a better path for growth.

So "build it and they will come" is only a valid approach if you have identified a solid demand for the product or service to be offered. You can't simply move into new quarters or create a new product in the hopes that a market's going to show up. You need to take the time to do your research and thoroughly analyze the realities of any assumptions you're making. Even though there's always some risk involved in any product or business launch, this level of analysis and research can help you better understand your business' infrastructure needs and put you in much better control of your odds for success.

Nonprofits Facing the Plateau

CovingtonAlsina is a typical situation, where owners/founders approach me for help thinking they have already identified the problem, but they are not sure how to resolve the issue and move forward. In most cases, the inhibitors are a combination of internal and external factors. For some organizations, like nonprofits, decisions by management are also complicated because the organization is run by a board of trustees. In these cases, problems arise because many times managers and boards of trustees are both in position to make decisions from very different perspectives. The nonprofit organizational design is setup to provide checks and balances in decision making and to theoretically protect the organization. Management and staff frequently provide a front line, operational perspective, while the trustees operate from a volunteer, more big picture perspective. When it works, it can help balance needs, opportunities, and risks. When it doesn't work, it can severely limit the scope and success of the nonprofit organization and mission.

This happens more often than you might suspect. It isn't at all unusual to find that the trustees, as part-time volunteers, are mostly concerned about ensuring that nothing goes wrong on their watch. This frequently means that there is no ambitious seeking of opportunity and no expansion of scope and vision. Management staff is passionate about what the organization delivers, but makes most decisions from a perspective of the day-to-day, not the longer term.

I know of one such nonprofit that fell into this trap. The long time Executive Director became frustrated with changes that the trustees were pursuing. He did not see how the new vision being put forward by his board would benefit the current status quo. He chose to resign. This sent the trustees into a panic and they scrapped their new vision and went about looking to hire a replacement who would continue with the old mission and shore things up. The trustees conducted a panicked search and found a new Executive Director whose resume seemed perfect for the old role.

In the meantime, the opportunities that had convinced the trustees to originally change the vision and scope of the organization began to find other outlets. The new Executive Director stepped into a situation where the organization was severely shaken, while the promising opportunities that had precipitated this had been ignored or rebuffed. This ED found herself without many options, while being asked to take the nonprofit back to its previous heights based upon its old stale mission.

The ED tried, but didn't possess the skills to reinvent. She had been hired to replace and replicate the old ED, whose skills were not entrepreneurial either. The nonprofit was in danger of folding completely. The new ED was fired by the trustees as the organization was collapsing. The trustees now began to debate what to do to salvage the situation. Some of the trustees wanted to do away with the position of ED altogether. After all, it was the previous EDs that had gotten them into this jam to begin with and the trustees could surely run the organization better themselves. Another group wanted to approach the original ED and ask him back.

Thankfully, these trustees didn't prevail. More level headed trustees stepped in and did what should have been done to begin with. Instead of panicking and trying to go back in time with their hiring plan, they elected to first determine what the nonprofit's vision and scope should be. They then went about hiring for this need, not hiring based upon panic or hiring for a past need that was no longer the organization's reality.

Another similar example is a nonprofit arts organization that started becoming less relevant to their constituents and found that they couldn't continue to accomplish the good they were once able to with only a volunteer staff. They came to the realization they needed to invest in bringing key paid staff into the organization in order to take it in new directions. It was important, the trustees saw, that in the end, the organization could end up disappearing completely if changes were not made.

At this point, they made an important decision as a board. They decided they needed to hire a paid manager for the organization. If they were able to justify hiring musicians, conductors, and marketing firms, there was no reason why they shouldn't be able to hire a manager to keep the organization growing in the right direction. Having someone with experience sitting in the main office, responsible for keeping everything together, had become important and this board was wise to recognize that fact. Getting someone in a position to monitor the bigger picture, helping with the marketing and creating a presence for the organization was a key component to the whole undertaking and a Managing Director could help handle all those key components and get the organization headed on the path to attaining their goals.

They ended up hiring a woman who had a lot of credentials. She sounded almost too good to be true, and she was available. They happily closed the deal and got her on board and working. Even though it seemed like a brilliant move, it ended up being awful. The woman they hired failed to deliver and the organization floundered. Ultimately the community suffered because the bad decisions of the new manager negatively affected the good that the organization was hoping to do. The pressure continued mounting and the woman they'd hired ended up disappearing. She simply didn't show up to work one day. The damage she did during her brief tenure was bad enough, but the real danger for anyone in a similar situation is the effect this kind of experience can have on future hiring. The organization looked at the entire episode as a disaster and didn't know what to do. They'd hired a woman with the best of intentions and credentials to back her up, but nothing worked out as the organizers expected or intended. It was such a bad overall experience that they didn't want to go through anything like that again.

In reality, that mindset was their worst enemy in the situation. Certainly, they should have recognized there was a problem that needed to be corrected earlier, and this was compounded when a mistake was made in the hiring process. They needed to do better in their hiring and find someone who could handle what the other hire could not. The last thing to do was shy away from finding someone else, because the first experience went badly. After all, the organization still needed someone to fill that role and the need wasn't going to go away on its own.

Strategic Hiring

This is why careful business analysis and development, which includes planning how to handle the unexpected, is so crucial for small business as well as large. You can't let the fear of making a mistake bring you to a halt - you will make mistakes. There are always reasons to stall when it comes to important decisions and few will come with as many uncertainties as adding key personnel, but stalling isn't going to get your business past the plateau before it's too late.

This is where hiring a business development professional can make a huge difference – but finding and hiring the right one for your specific needs can be dicey, too. You have to determine what a realistic timeframe is for the individual to deliver on his or her promises. You need to know that if this person isn't working out for you within a specified timeframe, you can move on to someone else and still get the job done with minimal interruption.

Too many businesses are trying to bootstrap their growth with only the in-house resources they have available to them. An experienced business development professional, who successfully practices their craft for your business, can provide good ROI by providing additional resources to help you afford additional personnel. Set things up so that, if something isn't working, you can easily move on. Establish a trial period of a couple of months to evaluate potential permanent employees. Ensure that the appropriate language is in any personnel contracts, and that your own mindset is open to relieving any candidate that fails to meet needs or expectations.

Once you clarify your needs and are capable of successfully hiring key personnel from a strategic standpoint, you'll find it's the ideal way to run your business, even during those times when it feels like an expense you can't afford. Do it in a comprehensive but prioritized fashion by filling positions in your departments most in need of fresh eyes, additional talent, and experience. Keep to this strategy as long as you can muster the resources to do so. If you stick with this, adjusting quickly when one hire doesn't work out, you'll soon find more and more resources available to you to continue the process. You'll be better equipped to push through the inevitable plateau and into real high growth.

Arts Council of Anne Arundel County I: Organizational Redesign

The Arts Council of Anne Arundel County is a large agency in Maryland providing funds for the arts. The agency experienced an unexpected crisis when the Executive Director was forced to step down for health reasons. This crisis led to a complete reassessment of their purpose.

Glitches, sometimes major – like the unexpected exit of someone who is perceived to be irreplaceable - is something experienced by many small businesses/ organizations. Sometimes glitches lead to positive change in a big way, as was the case when the Arts Council brought in April Nyman as the new ED.

I had started volunteering with the Arts Council some months earlier and had eventually joined the board. When April stepped in as Executive Director, I assumed the position of President of the Board and worked with her hand-in-hand to move the organization beyond its current plateau.

The ED April replaced was long-established and well-loved, a situation that can make for a difficult transition period. Similar to the complexities of Ann's financial planning business, April needed help with a number of issues – not the least of which was a typical following-a-founder situation. She had a much more expansive vision of what an Arts Council could be and do than previous leadership had ever considered. After April's hire, she and the Board started launching the initiatives and making the plans to bring her vision into reality.

"The Council recognized, by hiring me, that my vision was much larger and they indicated that they wanted to go after it," she said, "but it was very hard for them to let go of the 'this is the way we always do it' attitude. I had to wait for some board members' terms to expire, so we could bring in some new blood."

This type of challenge is common, especially with organizations trying to get beyond their founder's vision – or where their founder left it. It's actually rare for the person who immediately follows the founder to have as much success as April experienced. April and I worked strategically, matching vision with organizational direction and personnel. We were constantly looking at who would be leaving the board, who would be the best replacement, and the dynamics of who would be on which committees to ensure progress toward our goals. We wanted to avoid any road blocks. It wasn't that we were making all the decisions. We were evaluating the makeup of the board, actively working with current members, and recruiting new members with the skills and vision to help us make the right decisions.

My role as Board President included putting together a leadership team on the executive committee that would help guide board development. The person who was my Vice-President was also in charge of the governance committee. She's someone I've worked with in other organizations, who knows the drill very well and is very good at being, for lack of a better term, the accountability lady and the bearer of bad news. She's very good at holding everybody's feet to the fire to accomplish the organization's goals.

The Arts Council is a classic example of how having key personnel in your organization is essential, and how it can be accomplished, whether as a for-profit organization or a nonprofit. Lacking key people in decision making positions can substantially inhibit businesses' potential to grow. Conversely, if you get the right people, you have to give them the space and time to allow them to do the job you are paying them to do. This is another key piece of the personnel puzzle.

Right from the start, April had to contend with the Jack-of-all-Trades Mentality. She was being micromanaged by the board and was responsible for everything, with only part-time help and volunteers to assist. Nonprofits are notorious for minimal pay, so finding the right person is frequently the first challenge and keeping them any length of time – especially in a secondary position – is a significant challenge. It is always difficult to allocate funds to add staff when you're strapped. But, if you get the right staff in, they help you generate money and help you become more efficient.

In the case of the Arts Council, we were able to use specific program money to seed some additional staff members. These staff members, who possessed specific skill sets and were assigned specific duties, proved the value in having adequate staff. Suddenly, the board was happy to find the funding to keep these folks on, thinking, "We can't let that hire go. We've got to keep them."

The Technology Inhibitor

Aside from recruiting the right people to effect change, businesses in general, and the Arts Council specifically, need to address another huge infrastructure piece of the puzzle: technology. Technology is the most neglected and overlooked opportunity for both businesses and nonprofits. If anything tech-related has been done the same way for the last three to five years, there's an opportunity being missed. Technology can be a rapidly changing internal inhibitor to business growth.

Many small businesses think of technology as a few networked computers, a phone system, and a few other industry-specific tech tools. The ability of these businesses to keep up with changing trends in technology is awful, because the acquisitions weren't made with the right kind of planning prior to making the purchase. Most technology is chosen and put into place to support current systems. Rather than seeing technology as a tool that can help grow the business, it is often looked at as a one-time expense, with upgrades being a low priority.

This is a short-sighted approach, as technology is continually changing and should be viewed as an opportunity. Technology and the overall company infrastructure need to be routinely monitored, analyzed, and upgraded or improved, or you could easily find your company generations behind your competition and the market you are serving.

That doesn't mean you have to always have the latest, fastest hardware and most current software, but the fact is, you're missing out on possibly vital innovations happening all around you if you don't carefully monitor your technology and infrastructure with a plan for growth in mind. Your ability to deliver quality products and services, to interface with your clients, and to most effectively tap the resources of your vendors and your inventory, is constantly changing, thanks to new and upgraded technology. Technology can be the single greatest differentiator for any organization when designed and implemented properly.

If you do look up and find that you're several generations behind in technology and your growth has outstripped your infrastructure, you'll find an easy and inexpensive solution is very hard to come by. At this point, you might feel a crushing need to try and catch everything up and get back on track – but, now, you're having difficulty justifying the entire expense involved. You're forced to make vital decisions concerning which particular pieces of your business get upgraded first. It's easy to make the wrong choice when it comes to many of these decisions. You might find out, for example, that the version of the database you're currently running isn't even supported anymore and an update is required. In some cases, those updates may require an upgrade to your operating system as well. Realizing you didn't budget for the funds to do all that, you're forced to figure out alternatives.

This is the beginning of a defensive phase I call stop-gapping. You're still going to fall behind, but at a slower pace than what you were prior to stop-gapping. Instead of taking advantage of all the opportunities you have in front of you, while you have the resources to do so, and buying to fit a solid plan, you cobble together something that will stop-gap your needs. Ultimately, by this methodology, you still lose out in the end. For example, since you're falling behind in technology you're going to lose money. The more you lose, the less you have to work with to stay on top of new technologies. You could end up stop-gapping your way to being passed up by competitors.

Small businesses have to prioritize their technology and supporting infrastructure, in a way that makes it possible to stay on top of how changes and the growth of the business itself, are going to impact every aspect of operations and avoid the hamster wheel at all costs. You probably know the hamster wheel is quite addictive. Once business owners climb on the wheel, they tend to stay on it. They keep running in place while they speculate about what would happen if they were to get off the wheel.

Constantly evaluate new technology that might present a solid opportunity if it's incorporated into your business operations. As much as technology is continually changing and as broad as overall organizational infrastructure needs tend to be, budgeting to account for periodic technology upgrades is key to allow the business to grow and remain competitive.

Arts Council II: Technology Upgrade

The Arts Council is one such organization that repeatedly fell into using a stop-gap approach. April expressed frustration with her attempts to keep up with the organization's technical infrastructure. "We would try to do it in a small way and do it with the staff we had – and we would get everything all updated, then... nothing. Nobody updated things for a while or you let things go, and then you're back to right where you started." April found she really had to come up with a plan and have staff support the plan, or outsource the tasks, to take advantage and realize the potential that technology offered.

April's plan allowed the Arts Council to go from paper and pencil grant processing and a terribly outdated placeholder website, to a new online grant system with public access, online grant applications, and a brand new website with back office capabilities for replacing the paper and pencil record keeping methods. Follow up requests or comments can also be submitted online, diminishing processing time and improving processing efficiency. Applicants also get a history of their grant while the Arts Council is allowed use of the grantee's information for statistics and advocacy. This allowed the Arts Council to better work through their business plan, tracking the big picture to help keep their goals on track, now and into the future.

Another factor impeding the Art Council's success was marketing, an external inhibitor for many organizations. In April and my discussions on infrastructure, which involved personnel and technology changes, we found ourselves using the word "impact" often. How can we impact the arts in the county? How can we make our goals and objectives happen? In our own way, we were trying to identify our market and brand. Specifically, what are our clients/customers' needs and how can we fill them?

The previous director had gotten the organization to a stable place, but it was still very passive: we were funded, we would evaluate organizations, and then we would pass funds through to them. A nifty thing about a nonprofit is that the mission – unlike in a for-profit business – is number one. Financial performance, to a certain point, is number two. This gave us the ability to focus more on impact, to drive everything and move the organization from being passive to being more directly involved in the community. We had to expand our market and make that market aware of our value.

Rebranding

April and I spent a year with a marketing committee and hired an ad agency that put together a new website, with our guidance. We told them what we needed and what we wanted to accomplish with our new interactive site. We realized that because we were growing and our vision had changed so much, we needed a new brand or identity. We wanted a larger presence in the community's mind. We went from having a blasé logo, with no tagline, to a fresh new logo with the tagline: "Gateway to the Arts," quickly summing up the new Arts Council vision.

To successfully rebrand your own business, you must first determine what, if any, impact your current brand is having with your stakeholders and your market. Let's assume there are some elements of the company or organization that project the brand and are recognized within the market being served. The longer the brand sits in a plateaued position, the less fresh that brand is. This may be fine – going back to that high growth-versus-lifestyle approach – if your goal is to assure your clients that it's business as usual with you, that you're tried-and-true. You want to maintain the status quo. But, if you're looking to inspire people around the language of opportunity, you need a brand that says so. Ignoring the status of the brand in the marketplace could lead to disastrous results.

Know Your Market

One of the best examples of ignoring the marketplace is Schwinn Bicycles. Schwinn dominated the bicycle industry through most of the 20th century. Unfortunately, they took their eye off the ball and weren't paying attention to trends which clearly indicated the kinds of bicycles their consumers wanted most. As bicycling began changing from being a leisure activity into an exercise activity – even an extreme sport - other companies began selling mountain bikes in growing numbers.

Because Schwinn apparently was not adequately monitoring or tracking the client culture in the market they depended on, they ended up missing out on the mountain bike trend that many other companies capitalized on. Schwinn's factories weren't able to adapt quickly enough to make the changes required for production of mountain bikes, so they were unable to create the new and innovative products the market was demanding.

Schwinn went bankrupt in 1992, largely because they hadn't actively listened to their customers and their marketplace. Today, Schwinn is still producing bikes, but the company is operating as a sub-brand of Pacific Cycle, owned by multinational conglomerate Dorel Industries. The new incarnation of Schwinn sells bikes for more than just leisure – including a line of mountain bikes – but the company has never been able to re-establish the dominance it once held over this lucrative market.

Ignoring external changes, in Schwinn's case, was the root cause of the problem and was exacerbated by the failure of an internal company function. An external event – the market changes that were ignored – brought about the resulting impact, but the magnitude of the effect was guaranteed by the ineptness of the company. The internal problem that prevented seeing the coming market changes was the most important factor in the bankruptcy. For some reason, Schwinn's leadership was lacking or ignoring key information, when they analyzed the market, to assess what was going on around them. External factors directly contributed to Schwinn's woes to be sure, but ignoring those factors is what made things turn out as badly as they did.

Staying abreast of external factors, like changes in the demand for products or services, requires diligent work by business owners and/or personnel to manage a company's product/service presentation. A crucial part of this management is the constant need to measure consumers' responses to the products in the marketplace.

An example of a company monitoring consumers' pulse to determine demand is 3M. Started as a mining company in 1902, today 3M is an ergonomics company with annual sales of $30 billion. They were able to roll with the changing world to achieve incredible successes. They leveraged their resources and kept their people, infrastructure, and position in the industry as a thriving enterprise. They maintained a careful eye on trends and maintained their relevance in areas where a gap was present. This carried them through several different incarnations – from mining, to magnetic tape, to a variety of ergonomic products for today's marketplace.

Not every company is able to quickly adapt and innovate. Sometimes it is just too hard to see the opportunities for what they are. Gatorade originally pitched their electrolyte replacing sports drink to PepsiCo. It was brought in as a potential addition to Pepsi's line of soft drinks. The product was foreign to Pepsi, in regards to how soft drinks were made and what technology was needed. The company had difficulty understanding the vision of a non-carbonated sports drink. Pepsi couldn't get beyond their status quo. A sports drink didn't seem relevant to their business at the time so they elected to pass on a purchase of Gatorade. As luck would have it, Pepsi didn't have to fully experience how damaging a decision this could have been, long term. In 1983, Quaker Oats purchased Gatorade and then themselves were bought by PepsiCo in 2000. Gatorade is now Pepsi's fourth largest brand.

Challenging the Status Quo and Rising to the Challenge

This is an excellent example of what I call being forward-facing. Often, dealing with a single product line or category won't let you see beyond the inevitable plateau you'll face, if you aren't facing it already. By not opening up your possibilities, you could be missing out on something that could take your business to an entirely new level, above and beyond the plateau – possibly avoiding it altogether.

A willingness to step outside of your comfort zone is necessary if you want to harness opportunities that simply wouldn't be there otherwise. This can feel very uncomfortable. It might make sense to test things at a level that's closer to what you're already doing, so you can ease your way into something new for your business. Pepsi could have very easily retooled some systems and ramped up for Gatorade production - testing the market before overcommitting – but they couldn't see a fit or the potential.

Let's look at an example of a company being blindsided by outside negative forces and how a disaster was overcome. In 1982, seven people in Chicago died after taking Tylenol capsules that had been laced with potassium cyanide. The poisonings were headline news everywhere and quickly brought sales of Tylenol to a screeching halt, forcing shares of the company to plummet in value. The incident, which happened as a result of a criminal act outside of the company's control, hurt them severely in the short-term. But the company's response following the tragedy propelled them to even greater heights than what I'm certain they imagined they would ever again attain.

Tylenol quickly announced new anti-tampering packaging and its parent company offered a $100,000 reward for the capture and conviction of the perpetrator. Although no suspects were ever charged with the poisonings, federal anti-tampering laws followed and the company managed to regain its stature, largely due to the swift action they took to address the situation. As the Tylenol example proves, internal reactions to external factors are a lot more important than the external factors themselves.

Expanding your business into new markets can help achieve high growth. Sometimes, this can be done by altering your marketing, to aim existing products or services to new prospects. Other times, you have to be open to new product or service categories that will appeal to customers in other markets or to your existing customers.

If you can't bring yourself to change when the opportunity presents itself, you'll be limiting your growth potential. Period. All it often takes is one new skill, one new product, or identifying one new market segment to exploit, to start growing your business and blast past the plateau.

Arts Council III: Results

In the case of the Arts Council, its mission was outdated and its market focus too narrow to effect the impact it wanted on the community. It had a very bureaucratic-looking brand that was appropriate for a different age and was designed to answer outdated community needs. To get people to recognize its contemporary relevance and to acknowledge there's something going on at this Arts Council that's different and trendy, it needed to better project it. The redesigned brand reflects the organization's new energy and desire to have impact. In addition, the Arts Council began to reach out to new constituents, including artists. Before, the council was simply funding the organizations within which the artists worked. Now, there's significant outreach directly to the artists all because the Arts Council evaluated its market and re-branded to address the community's needs.

With all this new activity and the new initiatives, there's more press and more people are taking notice. They're saying, "Hey, this is interesting, who is this group? What's this about?" And they go to the website, which is now so cutting edge and sharp-looking, it's truly an arts website. It immediately legitimizes the council.

A salient point to remember here is, the Arts Council experienced more than just a brand transformation. It was an organization that didn't have a vision statement – only a mission statement. Now, there's a new vision statement accompanying the visuals on the website, personnel motivated and invested in the Council's vision, updated technology, and a brand new marketing package. This package includes the new logo and a tagline, where one never existed before. It has graphic appeal in addition to appropriate written content. Pulling all these aspects together and launching the rebranding at the right time, has a snowball effect as each effort supports the other. Another tell tale sign of the Art Council's success came in the form of an offered opportunity to manage an arts and entertainment district in the city of Annapolis - something the previous Arts Council board would never have touched.

Today, not only does April have two full-time staff members who each bring their own skill sets and have their own responsibilities, she's also outsourced more mundane tasks that she used to juggle herself. For example, a bookkeeping firm handles the financial work, eliminating the need for April and the board treasurer to spend hours a week pouring over records. There's been additional outsourcing on the website and social media. The new Arts Council is an excellent example of an organization that got away from the Jack-of-all-Trades Mentality by retaining experts to help identify the organization's internal and external inhibitors and strategically implementing action to address them.

It often happens that when critical components within a successful organization align themselves, the company or organization's finances are positively impacted. Despite being a mission driven nonprofit, an additional bonus to its re-visioning work was that the Arts Council's budget tripled – and the main source of funding is more secure than it was previously. The work that April led to transform the Arts Council was a success on multiple levels.

Market Demographics and Communications

CovingtonAlsina and The Arts Council of Anne Arundel County are excellent examples of organizations who faced multiple challenges to propel themselves into growth after experiencing a plateau. Businesses whose infrastructure is aligned with a strategic marketing analysis and plan, a plan which considers consumer demand and perspective along with market demographics, are better positioned to launch or re-launch themselves.

It is important to examine where your company fits into the marketplace. You also need to determine how to effectively communicate within the markets you're addressing. This is where defining the branding, advertising, and authentic capacities of your business comes into play.

Think about the immense marketing obstacles, due to outside forces, currently faced by the oil and gas industry. This is an industry made up of a number of huge companies that all now recognize that their size, the amount of profit they generate, and their relevance to the market has only a finite time remaining – although they don't know the timeline for certain. They're making mighty strides, doing everything they can to become known as energy companies, rather than oil companies.

BP, for example, now refers to itself as an energy company. Surveys show, however, that not many people accept or recognize this distinction. The public still largely recognizes BP as an oil and gas company. Whatever they might or might not be doing in the overall energy sector besides oil and gas, people aren't identifying them as being part of that market sector. The public doesn't yet care whether they're classified as an energy company or an oil and gas company and BP, despite spending huge amounts of marketing and public relations dollars, still hasn't maneuvered itself effectively to reach the point where people see them as an energy company.

It's virtually the same for all the companies in this sector. I'm certain these companies, seeing the writing on the wall, are doing a lot more than simply saying they're now working on other technologies. They are in fact, for all practical purposes, energy companies. Still, it is a difficult position for the company to assume and advocate, because of their history and the public perception attached to it.

When you hear the name Philip Morris, what immediately comes to mind? Cigarettes most likely. Once cigarettes became recognized in the United States as a health hazard, sales of tobacco products began decreasing, leaving Philip Morris trying to diversify their offerings so that they were not totally reliant on tobacco product sales. The company had already begun branching into other areas before the surgeon general's warning, investing their profits into other often-unrelated industries and markets. Even though Philip Morris branched into other areas, they were still essentially known to the public as a tobacco company.

In one way or another, Philip Morris has owned or controlled Kraft Foods, General Foods, and the Miller Brewing Company. It no longer even goes by the name of Philip Morris, having changed its name to Altria Group, Inc. in 2003. The Philip Morris brand, now a subsidiary of Altria Group, is still a market leader in the tobacco industry, both in the U.S. and abroad, but the company has dealt with a lot more than cigarettes for a number of years.

As you think about your own marketing and positioning, consider what might need to be changed to keep you moving forward. Is it the company's message? The public's perception? Is it your product or service? Like Ann's financial planning business, you have to ask if you're filling a gap. Or conversely, are you selling for a perceived need that doesn't need filling at this time? Are you selling into an area of demand that you're able to address better than your competitor(s)? Or are you selling a specific product or service that applies to a market niche that has little competition? These are very different situations and the answers will dramatically affect the positioning of your company and the marketing messages you must deliver.

If you're lucky, you might hit a homerun with a single product or service right from the start. Others might have to work at it a little harder. Once you have a product area that's doing amazingly well, it may be easy enough to sit on your laurels, stop growing, and keep the profits rolling in. However, it's often success in one market that allows far easier expansion into other markets, sometimes by simply adjusting your marketing message to that new audience.

External forces, like your industry's market and consumer demands, combined with infrastructure and the right key personnel – need to be monitored, nurtured, and updated on a regular basis to keep a business thriving.

The Capacity Inhibitor

Capacity is a poorly understood concept. It affects everything in your business. Capacity is the total amount of production under optimum conditions that each component of your business could realistically and consistently deliver. You have to establish the capacity of upper level management, in addition to your capacity to fulfill orders and run operations. How much does the organization depend upon upper management? If these individuals aren't performing adequately, does anything get done? If the key leaders aren't in the business, making decisions, pushing people to do their jobs, will things happen? You have to determine how much battery power, in the form of leaders, the business will require to grow and be successful. It is this information that has to be factored into the equation, along with operational effectiveness that determines what the organization is capable of.

One of the main factors you may face, as you map out your business' trajectory, is that your business has an excellent bottom line assessment of what it will take in terms of money, vendors, and personnel, to attain a specific size. The only problem is, it's easy to end up not taking into account certain more ephemeral factors. What is the capacity of the leaders, is your personnel aligned to the company vision, are all the stakeholders on the same page? In the end, you're unable to grow to your desired size and you can't understand why. Even though it looks do-able on paper, you'll continuously be buffeted with distractions. Your administrative systems are not designed or built for the same capacity as that of your production systems.

This mismatch is a huge problem for businesses of all sizes. Small businesses often aren't using any formulas in their formative years. Founders aren't putting their business through comprehensive systems analyses, above and beyond the financials, to ensure profitability. They're sitting back and deciding what they can and can't do by intuitive gut feelings. You must make certain you're aware of all the costs, monetarily and resource-wise, that are involved with each decision. Experts in this arena can help you utilize the best practices and business management formulas that need to be scrutinized in order to maximize the possibilities and minimize the risk. Illuminating the blind spots by sitting down and mapping everything out can make all the difference and a good advisor will be able to assist.

The owner needs to focus on time management. Understand you are only one person. If you find you must be present in the company for things to run smoothly, you need to plan how things should run when you aren't around. Determine the amount of productive capacity in use when you're not around. Determine if all your resources are allocated in a reasonable manner.

If most of the time, things don't run as smoothly when you're not around, and productivity hits a low point, you should take this as a clear signal your business is relying too much on your own time and abilities. You are behaving like a practitioner, not a business owner, whether you want to or not.

As a practitioner, you might say, "I know what I am and what I'm capable of and therefore, I'm going to open my office here and practice my profession." You open an office and go into practice. Clients come in and visit. At the end of the day, you can have the satisfaction of saying you own your own business, but in fact, you don't. What you own is a professional job you've created for yourself.

An alternate design might look like this. You have the skills required to handle your clients. You're capable of getting the job done for them. To be the owner of a business and not simply the owner of a professional job, however, you have to open up the same practice, take care of some clients and work to hire other professionals to do the job along with you. Before you know it, you'll have expanded to having three professionals working with you. Maybe then you'll only see clients 20 percent of the time, because you're busy planning the expansion of your business. Pretty soon, you can open another office or even two or three, without worrying about seeing clients at all. You're now the one managing the business itself, making sure it's properly taken to the next level. You are, effectively, a business owner.

Take your own time into account. Once you as the owner are aware of your time involved with the company and the limitations that imposes, you need to determine the same for key personnel. At what level will you need to add additional management in order to appropriately increase leadership capacity?

Also figure out what happens if things go wrong and put together contingencies. Most business owners fail to plan for this. Start highlighting the blind spots. Even if you aren't using the proper formulas, you can go by your gut and at least start thinking realistically about capacity measurements and what could happen to throw a wrench in the works. You'll be miles ahead in your quest to build a business that's truly poised for high growth.

While this might not sound like it has anything to do with your company, remember that business owners will almost always find themselves hitting a plateau. This is when you need to determine and recognize what your real motivation is for growing your business. If your motivation relies on the fact that you have a distinct set of skills that you enjoy using, you'll build your business as a practice – a professional job and not a high growth business – and your systems will reflect this. When your motivation comes, instead, from a desire to provide a solution that fills a gap in the market, independent of your personal skill set, you could well be building a business and your foundation should support that goal.

Winquest Engineering: Seeking Counsel

John Leitch launched Winquest Engineering Corporation in 2010 to service government contracts. He had a business partner with a lot of experience and contacts, and together, they spent roughly 18 months obtaining the clearances necessary to finally get rolling. They landed a contract and there was revenue, but when a federal sequester hit, John looked at what was going on with the federal budget and saw a looming problem. That's when he came to me to ask if I thought he should move his company into the commercial sector, to augment the government work they were already doing. I agreed wholeheartedly.

I introduced John to a contact who could be a potential catalyst to take Winquest in this new direction. "That's been a home run," John told me. "That gentleman is now our Director of Business Development and doing a fantastic job. It's just one of the many success stories of Winquest Engineering's involvement with Patrick and the Spark Business Institute."

To manage his budget as he expanded into new markets, I also suggested that John get creative and add people carefully, hiring as many as possible as 1099 contractors, with some incentives to sweeten the deal.

He followed my advice and, today, reports that his 1099 contractors are extremely excited. This is because John offers them the opportunity to acquire equity, when they demonstrate success in their positions.

I also suggested John seek some financing. I told him not to wait until he actually needed the funding to start the process. We found him a bank with particular expertise in government contracts. They were able to secure a significant line of credit for use as needed. In John's own words, "I thank Patrick and pat myself on the back for being smart enough to listen to him on that one."

As in both CovingtonAlsina and in recruiting board members for the Arts Council project, my focus for Winquest has been on finding key personnel. John and I have been working on this issue for more than two years, as a natural extension of how the business was set up. John agreed he would succeed or fail based on the foundation he built with the key people involved.

John said, "I'm the CEO. I'm the Chairman of the Board. I'm the treasurer. I'm the secretary. I'm the facility security officer. I'm the primary business developer and there are probably four or five other things I'm missing here." Initially demonstrating a true Founder's Cap and Jack-of-all-Trades Mentality, he realized after our discussions that he couldn't be responsible for all those activities. John is now outsourcing a lot of the more mundane tasks that used to fill his plate. The 1099 contractors he's brought on board and his business development manager are taking the business forward. "I've been able to work with my business developer," he said, "instead of having to do paperwork. This enables him to go out and get the next million dollar contract."

Examining his business' potential, his personnel needs, and his desire for outside advice, John recognized the need for more than one CEO-level brain to tap as he grew his business. "I attended a breakfast that Patrick, my outside business specialist, hosted and joined the private advisory board that he chaired, a long time before we even brought in our first revenue" he said. "There are a number of reasons I joined, in no certain priority order: one was access to expertise like what Patrick brings to the table. The second was accountability. It is one thing for me to go to my business partner and say, 'I didn't get done last week or last month what I thought I was going to do.' It's a whole different story to look around at your peers, who are in the same boat as you are, and say it. I wanted an unbiased sounding board where I could throw something out there and somebody could tell me, 'That's stupid. You're going to kill yourself if you do that.' Or, 'That's brilliant, go for it. I wish I'd thought of that.' Then, there are the networking opportunities, which have been fantastic – both with Patrick and with the group. Probably the last thing is keeping goals in sync. Making sure there's no imbalance between business and personal goals. I joined six months before we actually had revenue coming in. I never regretted it for a moment."

John's was actually a case of identifying plateaus before the plateaus came into existence, and this is how folks should approach their business model. One of the first and most important tasks when starting a business is to identify the goals and define a plan for reaching them: "Here's how I'm building this business. Here's where I expect my performance numbers to be." The plan should identify all the expected and potential obstacles out of the gate, and have options for addressing them to avoid the next plateau.

John went into his business desiring to build a high growth business and knowing full well the risks and sacrifices that would be needed to accomplish this goal. You might, as a business owner, feel it would be a bad thing to take the risks involved to go after high growth. Others may be quite comfortable with it. It is fine, if you feel staying where you are with your company is satisfactory – provided this is an informed and deliberate choice with consideration for your family, loved ones, employees, and customers. If the business owner and other major stakeholders are perfectly happy with the amount of money earned from the business at a given level, there is little cause for taking the additional risks necessary to realize more significant high growth.

Organizational Gravity

Now that you understand the inhibitors facing your business, you can start the process of assessing your own plateau and moving beyond it. How do you objectively determine where your business is right now and how to move it into a growth cycle?

The answer to this question boils down to an institutional approach, of sorts. You need to start thinking now about what you can do to continue exerting your impact with the least amount of personal hands on activity required. You have to think about your long-term role and your continued evolution as a business owner.

The following principles cover four of the components used in something I call "The Organizational Gravity Model." I utilize it with my clients, in addition to the analysis I've mentioned earlier, to help demonstrate the interdependencies of talent, brand, strategy, and culture. They'll provide your business with a good assessment of the necessary tools to help make sure it's ready to grow and capable of staying on-course – even through the inevitable plateau.

If you're unsure where your business is headed, you should ask yourself the following key questions, to determine whether you're on course for high growth or not:

Strategic Direction – Have you taken the time to revisit your growth strategy and how relevant it is to the marketplace on a yearly basis? Are you able to summarize this strategy for your company in less than 35 words? Do you and your employees both see this growth strategy in the same way? Your business should have a plan in place for getting everyone where they want to go for years to come. If you don't have a strategy for growth, you don't know how you're going to get anywhere.

Customer Satisfaction via Brand Relevance – Do you truly know what it is your customers value the most about your services and products? Do you know what they have to say about your brand? Once you know what makes your product amazing, can you harness that information and use it to grow and expand in ways you might not have thought about previously?

Cultural Alignment – Have you been able to embed a value-based culture into your business? Being able to deliver on the brand promise you have in place is important for gaining the attention of your customers. If you can't deliver on the promise of your brand, you'll lose the loyalty of your customers. You should be able to provide something for a wide range of different cultural groups, not just for one.

Leadership Accessibility – Are all the key leaders in the business accessible, available, visible, and approachable to all the individuals who work for you? Employees need to know they have someone they can turn to in any time of need. When employees don't feel as if they can gain access to someone who can answer their questions, it creates anxiety and frustration within the organization. Making sure someone can answer any issues that arise is imperative to making employees feel confident and secure.

Talent Gravity – Are you able to retain and attract the employees you need, to provide you with the support that will be required, in anticipation of your company's growth path? Beyond being able to retain the employees you currently have, you also need to be able to recruit qualified individuals to help fuel the further growth of your company.

Mindful Hiring, Recruiting and Transitioning – Are you targeting the right employees for your business? Are you able to bring in those who provide you with the best fit for the organization? Do you want to transition employees into a position where they can quickly become an effective contributor to the growth of your organization? The goal should be to bring on people who are capable of doing the most good for your organization to help you grow and flourish, so you operate an effective growth company.

Suitable Infrastructure – Do you possess an infrastructure and management process to help support and monitor the growth of the business in terms of sales, finances, technology, human resources, and other key components of the business? You don't want just one area to grow in the business. Rather, you need all areas growing, if you expect to achieve your long-term growth objectives.

Actively Influence Brand – Are you investing your money, time, and resources to actively influence and build your brand perception and establish what makes your business different in the marketplace? If you don't let people know what it is that makes your brand better than others in the market, people aren't going to spend their money buying from you. It's up to you to give them a reason why they should choose your product above all others.

Develop Managers and Leaders for the Next Generation – Does your business currently have a succession plan for supporting the anticipated growth of your business? How are you going to go about replacing key employees within the organization? Do you have a plan for developing managers and leaders, to make sure they're properly trained to perform the necessary duties? Beyond having key leaders for the business, you need to make sure they're trained properly and provided with the pertinent information to be successful in everything they do.

Frequent, Open, and Informal Communication Patterns – Do you and your management team demonstrate and look for frequent and informal dialogue with all the employees working for your business? Are you taking the time to try and speak with your employees? Do your employees feel comfortable coming to you with any issues they may have? You want all those working in the organization to feel as if they can talk to you about anything. The last thing you want is for employees to hide things because they're uncomfortable with or unable to access your key managers.

Reinvention – Are you actively pursuing and developing the products and services for the future, to enable a response to market trends or a change in the positioning of your company as a leader in the industry? The main goal is to create products that are keeping up with the changing times. If your products aren't the latest and greatest in the market, you'll find that people are increasingly going to head elsewhere to get what they need. It's important that you make the necessary changes in your business products and services to make sure you're always at the head of the industry.

A Culture of Growth and Learning – Are you responsive to the goals of those who work for you? Do you provide them with an opportunity to grow and develop in a number of areas that are the most meaningful to them, as well as the most contributory to your business? Employees should feel comfortable with the growth of the organization as you build it. They should be able to move up in the business, instead of staying in the same position year after year. Growth for your business is important to maintaining the happiness of your employees and happy employees will help your business grow.

Reasonable Compensation Packages – Do you currently have a compensation package that's equitable and fair for the job in which each employee is working? Do you recognize the performance of the employees and reward them accordingly? It's important that you're able to offer your employees a compensation package that's comparable to those your competitors offer. The last thing you want is to lose employees because you're not treating them as fairly as your competitors would.

Exit Readiness – In the event you were no longer around the business, would it continue to grow and operate without undue complications? You want to make sure your business is capable of doing everything it can to operate without a hitch, regardless of whether you're there to handle the daily operations or not.

Even though a number of companies will often talk about the above principles, some inevitably end up dismissing them as only something considered by people with extra time on their hands. Very few actively work at achieving all these goals. It's these goals – setting them and making them happen – that make the difference between a company that can achieve high growth and one that can't.

After all, you're far from the first person who ever started a company. As I said earlier, there are numerous resources at your fingertips to help you through the startup phase, both governmental and private sector. Once you've worked your way through the startup phase and you're a going concern, you need an outside viewpoint, one that you trust, to continue to help you. Someone who is able to look at your entire operation from the outside in, then to look at the product, the markets you serve, and your place in those markets, to help you identify and deal with new opportunities and challenges that arise.

An Owner's Motivations: The Key Factor

What type of owner will you find on The Great Small Business Plateau^{SM}? The most relevant issue right from the start is the inner motivation of the owner. Resolving this can be tricky. There are people who simply aren't suited to building a high growth business. They work hard to build a steady business with good revenue, hit the plateau and don't care to push harder to get through it and into real high growth. They should consider finding their business' equilibrium point and parking their venture there. There's no crime in that.

On the other hand, you could be the type of owner who is interested in building a business as large as possible. The motivation is there. You'll do whatever is required – with the same level of dedication to the task you poured into the startup phase – to push through to the high growth you desire.

Unfortunately, it's also possible to fool yourself into thinking you want to grow, when in reality, you would rather slow down and enjoy the lifestyle business you've built. At some point, many business owners reach a state where money isn't the main motivator any more. It's no longer the reason why they continue to run a business. They've gained a certain degree of comfort, prestige, and security. The primary goal has already been attained, so they feel changing the company in any major way isn't relevant. This lifestyle company is perfectly fine staying where it is and, as long as it doesn't start to see dwindling returns or face a major external event that affects revenues, there isn't a real need to risk anything. The company is already generating what it needs to in terms of payout and satisfying the owner's motivations.

Because so many business owners today have difficulty determining which kind of business is the best fit for them and the life they want to live, I almost always first devote a significant focus on helping with this analysis. Getting this right is crucial. Owners need to align their motivations to their stated goals and then match their behaviors to support these goals. Not every business owner is a high growth entrepreneur and those that aren't shouldn't feel anxiety over this truth. There's not much reason for a lifestyle business to bring in outside help, unless there's a specific correction needed to keep the ship on-course.

People who want a high growth business, however, need someone from outside to help them analyze their real motivations and move forward – or not – with an unbiased viewpoint guiding them. No one can help a lifestyle owner grow beyond the plateau. You can try putting them through the process, but you'll quickly find it's virtually impossible for it to work when the company's founder or owner isn't truly motivated in this direction. As soon as things start to get rough, the motivation is lost since remaining at a lifestyle business level really feels fine. It simply becomes too much effort to muster up the commitment to go for real high growth. This is where you may need help, identifying your business' equilibrium point, and optimizing your systems, so that you stay away from the unsustainable plateau and get maximum benefit from your lifestyle business.

This is why, when working with a small or mid-size company, the first thing we do at The Spark Business Institute is a major assessment of the true motivations of the founder and/or owner of that business. We first need to make certain the people involved, are truly ready and properly motivated, to do what's required to overcome the plateau and attain high growth.

Getting past the plateau and into high growth requires that you are motivated and committed to reach this goal. You'll need to be fully willing to invest time, money and resources – ideally working with a qualified outside advisor who can guide you.

As you consider your motivation, ask yourself:

Does working the hours you're working and doing the jobs you're doing now, motivate you?

Are you comfortable with what you currently have and the lifestyle that it affords you?

Are you worried more about taking risks or about the future of your company?

Do you feel as if you have a lot of people who are depending on you and this responsibility is more important than growth?

Does risk make you more anxious than security?

To push past the plateau and reach sustainable growth for your business, you'll need to break through all these potential barriers with a genuine determination to grow. Your success will depend further on whether you truly understand your motivations and base your goals accordingly. Will you strive for high growth or a slow-growth but stable lifestyle business?

Considering the challenges, perhaps it should not be surprising that so few advisors and consultants currently serve the small business sector. It can be a frustrating process that, handled incorrectly, can be dangerous for the client. Ultimately, these business owners have a lot of resources tied up maintaining their current level. For many, they're struggling to manage even that. When an advisor steps in and asks them to reallocate their resources, he or she is asking the business owner to move into unfamiliar, potentially risky territory. Many business owners will resist the recommended changes. They might genuinely be confused about their true motivations, and with resources already tied up, getting them to move in a growth direction is difficult and often not necessary. This makes finding the ideal client difficult for business advisors serving this market.

Get Off the Plateau

For many business owners, this assessment will feel like when they first began their business. They'll reach a plateau, where it becomes obvious some extra effort or a new direction is required to move beyond that point. They will stay there for quite some time, while they try to think their way off the plateau. Eventually, it no longer feels temporary, but quite permanent. Even though it seems they should be able to figure out how to get out of the rut, it isn't working out that way. This leads to high levels of anxiety. At this point, business owners become open to the advice of qualified outside advisors and the ideas that others can bring to the table, to get them out of the rut they're now stuck in.

It is important for business owners to know that being on The Great Small Business Plateau^{SM} is not a sustainable place. They really have two choices, either to optimize their current systems and find their business' equilibrium point to allow for a successful lifestyle business, or to redesign the current business to blast past the plateau and head for high growth. Being honest about motivations, both personal and business, is a key first step for the owner. Outside guidance is frequently needed.

With or without outside guidance, if you're a motivated business owner and you're willing and able to tackle the decisions necessary to move the business beyond the plateau, you can do it. The observations contained in this book will help you get started. Good luck!

ABOUT THE AUTHOR

Patrick Lee is the CEO of the Spark Business Institute and President of the Chesapeake Think Tank. He has a Masters of Arts in Management with concentrations in Corporate Management and Business Communications from Notre Dame of Maryland University. He has practiced the art of entrepreneurship on more than one occasion, which included co-founding the Eastern Veterinary Blood Bank. He currently works with business owners to help them align their stated motivations with their actions. Patrick lives in Stevensville, Maryland with his wife and two children.

49054491R00061

Made in the USA
Middletown, DE
04 October 2017